SECRETS OF
SHAOLIN TEMPLE
BOXING

Figure 1 (frontispiece). Ta Mo, the transmitter of Zen from India to China: traditional father of Shaolin boxing.

SECRETS OF
SHAOLIN TEMPLE
BOXING

Edited by
Robert W. Smith

CHARLES E. TUTTLE COMPANY, INC.
Rutland, Vermont
& Tokyo, Japan

Representatives
Continental Europe: BOXERBOOKS, INC., Zurich
British Isles: PRENTICE-HALL INTERNATIONAL, INC., London
Australasia: PAUL FLESCH & CO., PTY. LTD., Melbourne
Canada: m.g. hurtig ltd., Edmonton

Published by the Charles E. Tuttle Company, Inc.
of Rutland, Vermont & Tokyo, Japan
with editorial offices at
Suido 1-chome, 2-6, Bunkyo-ku, Tokyo, Japan

Copyright in Japan, 1964 by Charles E. Tuttle Co., Inc.
All rights reserved

Library of Congress Catalog Card No. 64-22002

First edition, 1964
Second printing, 1968

PRINTED IN JAPAN

To Sidney Tai and Peter Chen

for help in guiding me through
the maze of Chinese boxing

Table of Contents

Editor's Foreword

THERE are no good books on Shaolin Temple boxing. There are only varying degrees of poor. Generally, they are repetitious rehashes of earlier legends. In Taiwan (1959–62) I was able to collect many personal manuscripts, and even these varied little from the low level of the published work.

One of my Shaolin teachers, Liao Wu-shang—he of the low skill—hearing of my plight, took me to a colleague, one Wang, the boxing "boss" of his area in South Taiwan. After several visits which protocol demanded, the old man with the outsized gnarled hands shared with us a short manuscript on Shaolin. His teacher from Shantung on the mainland had given it to Wang 40 years before. He believed that his grand-teacher had written it for his small circle of students and that few on the mainland and no one on Taiwan had ever seen it.

Subsequently, however, I learned that, while it was true that few on Taiwan had seen the book, it had been fairly widely known on the mainland. A leading boxing historian told me that originally the book had been a fine text but that Ch'en T'ieh-sheng, a Cantonese journalist, had amplified and distorted the work of the anonymous author. Later, other writers had added some of the ridiculous legends which abound in other popular books on Shaolin.

By this time I had had the work translated and was happily surprised to find parts of it enlightening. I believed that the points it stressed represented the core of Shaolin, the father of all boxing forms in China. And as I studied other sources in the boxing bibliography I kept coming back to this one.

With the current fad of karate in the West I felt that the grandfather ought to be known as well as its popular grandson. So I set about readying this book for publication in English. This involved deleting extraneous, repetitive, and legendary matter: editorial surgery I performed in an attempt to cut off the later additions grafted on the original by Ch'en and others. I hope that as it now stands it accords in some modest respect with the original.

Han Ch'ing-t'ang and Kao Fang-hsien, two of the leading Shaolin experts in Taiwan, posed for the illustrations—the original had none. Doug Bone, good friend and martial-arts cohort, also posed for some of the photographs. Another veteran boxer, Liang Tung-tsai, assisted me in interpreting parts of the text. Tai Lien, who did reams of translation for me for three years, provided a clear text. Liao Wu-shang and his colleague Peter Chen early on said they would get me a real book on Shaolin...and did. My warmest thanks to all these men I call friends.

Finally, old Wang. I never told this kindly gentleman that his treasured secret was not really very secret. The book had been the basis of his lifetime boxing. He was happy thinking he alone had it, and I saw no reason to impinge on a 40-year-old dream. This was my thanks to him.

ROBERT W. SMITH

Bethesda, Maryland

SECRETS OF
SHAOLIN TEMPLE
BOXING

1

A Brief History

THE term "Ch'uan" means the use of the fist(s). Though somewhat misleading, the art of boxing has been called "Ch'uan Fa" for generations. Actually the fist makes up but a small part of boxing. For example, in the Southern school the fist represents less than 10 percent of the 170 hand operations. Moreover, when we do use the fist it is more often than not done by means of unclenched fingers (for example, in the "Tiger's Claw"). A flat fist with the fingers clenched decentralizes the force of a blow and is therefore laughed at by veteran boxers.

Origins

Before boxing proficiency can be attained, the Five Styles handed down from Monk Ta Mo must be mastered. The learning of these soft methods goes to the core of the art: without it one remains forever a novice.

Monk Ta Mo lived during the Liang dynasty (A.D. 506–56). In teaching his Buddhist students he noted that the frail novices fell asleep during his lectures. Believing that a strong body would not only remedy this weakness but would also

bring one closer to his soul, he gave them a set of 18 actions to be done regularly each morning.*

The Eighteen Exercises

1. Stand upright, your waist straight, eyes wide open, and mind concentrating. Exhale the stale air and inhale the fresh.

2. *Stretch toward the Sky.* While holding the *ch'i* (intrinsic energy) down in the lower torso your left hand goes up, your right down alternately, your two palms open and flat. Two actions.

3. *Pushing the Mountain.* Following the preceding style, separate your feet about a foot and alternately push your palms directly forward. Strength is centered in the middle of the palms and your *ch'i* sinks to your navel. Four actions.

4. *Black Tiger Straightens Waist.* Stand upright and then squat in a low horse-riding posture. Stretch your palms out as you change into a high horse-riding posture. The centers

---

* The exercises given in the text are ambiguous and defy clear understanding. However, most authorities ascribe to Ta Mo authorship of the *I Chin Ching* (Muscle Change Classic), the exercises of which are not dissimilar to those listed. Only 12 of these 24 exercises, however, are believed to be the work of Ta Mo. These are included here along with the illustrations found in the oldest versions of this work. (ed.)

of your palms are linked for strength with your heels. This action will strengthen your waist. Four actions.

5. *Wild Goose Beats Wings.* Relax and rest a little. Then inhale and let your *ch'i* sink. Keep your hands close to your legs and draw strength from under your armpits. Your shoulders are held flat like the opened wings of a wild goose. Your heels rise and fall with the shooting out and retracting of your arms. One action.

6. *Lower Elbows and Hook Palms.* Stand upright and make a step forward with either your right or your left foot. Lower your palms gradually to your knees, simultaneously hooking your fingers. Depress your waist a little but keep strength in your elbows. One action.

7. *Draw the Bow and Brace the Diaphragm.* This is similar to "Drawing the Bow and Killing the Wild Goose" in the "Eight Boxing Methods." But in one the low horse-riding posture and in the other an upright posture is used. One action.

8. *Golden Leopard Reveals Claws.* In the preceding action the palm was used. In this exercise the fingers are hooked into a near fist. Use a medium horse-riding posture and a

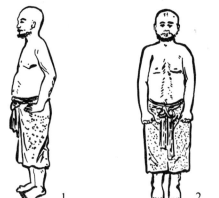  

Figures 2–4. Muscle Change Exercises 1–3.

shout as you attack. The strength comes from under your armpit. One action.

9. *Toe Kicking.* Keep the kick low. If too high you lose effect and can be countered. One action.

10. *Sweeping Leg.* Turn laterally and shoot out your leg in a sweep. After sweeping retract it quickly. One action.

11. *High Kicking.* This is very dangerous and leaves you susceptible to counter. Never use it unless you can do so speedily and well. One action.

12. *Hooking Leg.* Hook your foot in a small circle. One action.

The Muscle Change Classic

Each exercise is different with distinctive merits. Open space, good ventilation, and ample time morning and night are all that are required. After you learn the entire set of 12 do the whole three times in the morning and three times in the evening. If you persist in regular practice, in one year your health will improve greatly and you will be on the threshold of further physical and spiritual development.

1. Sink your *ch'i,* calm your mind, and concentrate. Separate your feet by one foot. The tip of your tongue goes to

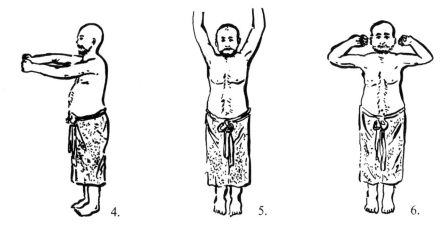

Figures 5–7. Muscle Change Exercises 4–6.

the juncture of your lower and upper teeth. Curve your arms slightly and raise the fingertips until your hands are horizontally fixed. As you curve your arms the strength goes down, pushed, as it were, by the base of your palms (as if you were placing your hands on a table preparatory to jumping). Do this slowly several times, relaxing and straining alternately. Then lower your fingers. (See Figure 2.)

2. Put your feet closer together than in the preceding exercise. Clench your fingers into loose fists but with the thumbs straight. Bring your fists in front of your loins, the thumbs on a line. Then raise your thumbs up as far as they will go. Hold a short while, relax and lower thumbs. Do 49 times. (See Figure 3.)

3. Again separate your feet by a foot. Your legs hold strength downward—they never relax. Fold your fingers over your thumbs and relax your shoulders. Tighten your fists. Do several times. This develops the fists and lower arms. (See Figure 4.)

4. Put your feet together. Close your fingers around your thumbs and raise your arms frontally until they parallel your shoulders. This focuses strength frontally. Do up to 39 times. (See Figure 5.)

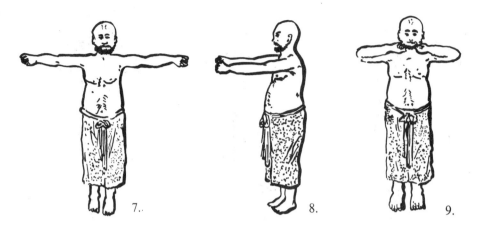

Figures 8–10. Muscle Change Exercises 7–9.

5. Your feet remain together. Raise your fists outward circularly, with the palms up, overhead until your fingers are parallel. Keep your arms curved slightly and as you raise your arms go up on your toes. After you raise your arms clench your fists tightly, then lower. This circulates *ch'i* throughout your body. Do 49 times. (See Figure 6.)

6. Separate your feet. Make normal fists, thumbs clenched over fingers. Raise your arms laterally, palms up until they parallel shoulder. Then bring the forearms up forming a triangle, your palms facing your shoulders. Clench fists tightly. Do 49 times. This strengthens elbows, wrists, and chest. (See Figure 7.)

7. Bring your feet together. Keeping normal fists, raise your arms frontally until they parallel shoulders. Using strength, take your arms to the direct side where they are aligned to your shoulders. Your palms are down. Then rise on toes and alternately stand on the heel of each foot. As you lower toes, exhale and open your fists. Do 49 times. This improves the internal environment. (See Figure 8.)

8. Your feet remain together. Your thumbs are covered by your fingers. Raise your fists frontally to shoulder level with the palms facing each other. As you raise your arms go

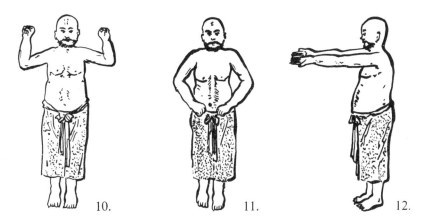

Figures 11–13. Muscle Change Exercises 10–12.

up on your toes. Then clench your fists tightly. Relax and lower heels. Do 49 times. This exercise trains the arms to draw *ch'i.* (See Figure 9.)

9. Your feet are still together and your fingers clenched around your thumbs. Raise your arms frontally but bend your elbows when your fists reach the level of your abdomen. Raise your fists, palms out, to face level forming a triangle. Then clench fists and turn forearms inward until palms face your face. Do 49 times. (See Figure 10.)

10. Your feet remain closed and your fingers clench your thumbs. Raise your arms frontally to shoulder height. Then carry your fists vertically and hold them with your palms facing the front. Hold your arms as if holding 1,000 pounds with elbows straining out and fists clenched tightly. Do 49 times. (See Figure 11.)

11. Your feet are close but your fists are now made with the thumbs clenched outside your fingers. Keeping your clenched fists relaxed, raise them to your navel. Your elbows are curved. Then clench your fists tightly with thumbs raised from them. Your strength feels as if it creeps up your arms. Then lower your thumbs and relax your fists. Do nine times. This exercise lets the *ch'i* rise and fall. Be sure to inhale

through your nose and to exhale just as you relax. (See Figure 12.)

12. Keep your feet close. Your fingers hang down at your sides with the palms outward. Raise your arms frontally to shoulder level. Hold your hands so that your thumbs face outward and your palms face the sky. As you raise your arms, rise on toes. Hold this posture a short while, then lower your arms and heels. Do 12 times. This exercise relaxes your sinews. (See Figure 13.)

Further Development

Thus started the so-called 18-Monk Boxing. Initially Ta Mo originated it solely for health. After his death his disciples dispersed and the art was nearly lost. Then during the Yuan dynasty (A.D. 1260–1368), a wealthy young man surnamed Yen became a priest and took the name Chueh Yuan. Interested in boxing, he revised Ta Mo's 18 methods into 72 styles and promoted the Shaolin art till it thundered throughout China.

But Chueh Yuan was not content with that. He traveled throughout the mainland searching out famous boxers to test their methods. In Lanchow of Kansu he came upon a

60-year-old peddler being manhandled by a big oaf. When the brute attempted to kick the dodging veteran, the old man touched his foot with two fingers of his right hand. The attacker fell unconscious. Chueh Yuan struck up an acquaintance with the veteran, whose name was Li Ch'eng. Li disclaimed any great knowledge of boxing but introduced him to a friend Pai Yu-feng of Shansi, reputedly matchless in Shansi, Honan, and Hopei.

Pai was 50, of a medium build, and radiated with spirit. Li, Pai, and Chueh Yuan went to the Shaolin Temple and there consolidated Ta Mo's 18 and Chueh Yuan's 72 movements into 170 actions which are the basis for our Shaolin today.

The Five Styles

The 170 actions were embraced in Five Styles: Dragon, Tiger, Leopard, Snake, and Crane. Pai taught that man has five essences: (a) spirit, (b) bone, (c) strength, (d) *ch'i,* and (e) sinew. These essences must be merged and synchronized into an efficient oneness. Included within is the synthesis of hard and soft, internal and external, and substantial and insubstantial.

DRAGON

(SPIRIT)

Figure 14. Dragon (Spirit).

The Dragon Style represents the cultivation of spirit. Strength is not used. The *ch'i* is centered in the navel and your body kept light and lively. Keep your shoulders balanced and the five centers (heart, two palms, and two feet centers) responding to one another. This movement resembles a dragon floating in the air capable of movement in every direction. (See Figure 14.)

The Tiger Style represents the training of the bones. Brace

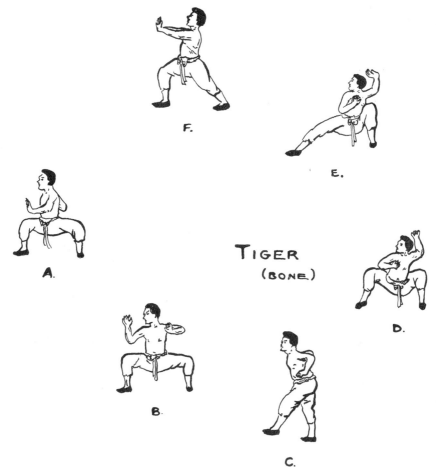

F.

E.

TIGER
(BONE)

A.

D.

B.

C.

Figure 15. Tiger (Bone).

yourself and hold your shoulders and waist firmly. Let your body rise and fall as your *ch'i* circulates and your two eyes are kept open. This movement resembles an angry tiger leaping out of the woods. (See Figure 15.)

The Leopard Style represents the development of strength. Though a leopard does not look so awesome as a tiger, it is able to generate greater strength. Because it likes to jump, its waist and lower extremities are stronger than those of a

LEOPARD

(STRENGTH)

A.
B.
C.
D.
E.
F.

Figure 16. Leopard (Strength).

tiger. Hooking your fingers into a near fist, brace yourself and sink and rise with a low horse-riding posture. (See Figure 16.)

The Snake Style represents the cultivation of *ch'i*. Do rhythmical inhalation and exhalation calmly. The snake's *ch'i* permeates his entire body so that when the snake touches anything it appears spongy and without strength. But it can draw instant strength like that of the strongest man. The

SNAKE
(CH'I)

Figure 17. Snake (Ch'i).

old saying: "The best steel can be used as a rope to tie around a pillar" exemplifies this style. Your whole body moves endlessly and is soft yet strong, flexible yet firm. Your two fingers are used like the tongue of a snake. (See Figure 17.)

The Crane Style represents sinew training. The sinew is rooted in the feet but the spirit permeates throughout the body. Your shoulders are always kept relaxed, and your

CRANE

(SINEW)

Figure 18. Crane (Sinew).

hands and feet harmonize. Your will must be tranquil and your mind far-reaching. (See Figure 18.)

The mastery of the Five Styles requires tedious effort and endurance. But when it comes your body will become sturdy, your limbs firm, your eyes sharp, and your courage great. When you encounter an enemy a finger or a foot can win the fight.

The North and South Schools

Generally, the boxers of the North are hardier than those of the South. The climate there is more severe, the conditions of life more stringent, and the food more conducive to strength. Moreover, most of the great Northern boxers have worked as armed escorts for goods convoys: an excellent if dangerous profession in which to test their boxing prowess.

2

The Basis

Ch'i

There are many schools teaching the "soft" form of the martial arts. All begin and end with *ch'i,* or intrinsic energy. To master this energy is to pierce the unknown and to reach the state where life and death lose their qualities of fear. When you achieve this a threat does not disturb nor a temptation caress. You become true master of your self. Many there are who constantly murmur magic words about *ch'i* but who react to an emergency with frantic fear. They merely talk: they have done nothing about *ch'i.* For this reason our art is deteriorating.

There are two aspects of *ch'i.* You must first cultivate it and then exercise it. When the energy is cultivated it is held in balance inside your body. Thus your mind is tranquilized and every movement becomes graceful and harmonious. When this is achieved, you may then talk about how to deal with an enemy. Confucius stressed *ch'i.* In order to defeat an enemy, the boxing art cannot do less.

Ch'i is cultivated without conscious effort. By conscious breathing it is exercised. Practice dwells on exhalation and inhalation. The initial process is from soft to hard but later

Figure 19. Horse-riding Posture   *Figure 20.* Horse-riding Posture: Application

you must reverse the process, thus returning from hard to soft. Successful boxing combines the soft and the hard. It is important to be soft with the insubstantial and hard with the substantial. While you are soft on the right side you must be hard on the left. This may puzzle you, but it will become clear as we progress. Monk Chueh Yuan stated:

> Strength turns from soft to strong and *ch'i* becomes substantial from cultivation. Strength originates from *ch'i* and acts as *ch'i* sinks. Without *ch'i* there is no strength. A quack boxer shoots out a hand ferociously, but there is no true strength in his strike. A real boxer is not so flamboyant, but his touch is as heavy as a mountain. This is because he possesses *ch'i*. Through long practice all the *ch'i* can be focused on the attacking point. The will commands the *ch'i* which can be focused on any given point instantaneously.

1. *The Foothold.* In exercising the *ch'i* you must first practice the foothold exercise. You first stand in the horse-riding posture, which will permit rapid rising or dropping (Figures 19 and 20). This posture is excellent in that it makes the

loins and legs durable and the entire body stable. With it you can stand firmly, even on a precipice.

After assuming this posture you should direct the *ch'i* to your lower torso. Do not let it float in the chest. If you do, your upper part will be heavier and you cannot root your feet to the ground. Many there are who will fall at the slightest push. This is because they have not practiced the hold exercise.

An old saying goes: "Before you can learn to defeat others, you must first learn to stand." After you have learned how to stand firmly, your *ch'i* is always kept just below the navel, enabling you to achieve a strong foothold at any time or place. Then and only then are you ready to learn boxing.

At first in the foothold training you may feel some ache in the loins and legs. It is like riding a horse after a long interval. You may also feel a weakening of your strength. But do not worry. This merely means a washout of the old. All worthless air and useless strength a novice possesses before training have to be replaced by the new. Thus, when you feel pain initially, do not flinch but, instead, endure the pain and continue practicing.

In order to learn the foothold you must increase the standing time each day. For example, if you practice two hours* the first night, add several minutes the next. Progress must come every day. If the leg pains are unbearable you may rest a short while, but then return to the posture. You must stand every day until the pain vanishes naturally with the sinking of your *ch'i* to your lower navel and the onset of strength to your legs. Only then can the hands be trained. At first, you should direct your *ch'i* from your armpits to your fingertips. Later, you can direct the entire body strength toward and through the hands. Then you will feel that your entire body and its extensions, the hands and feet, will act in concert. Your sinews will be activated and your blood circulation promoted. Your body will then respond perfectly to your slightest demand.

2. *Breathing.* The lungs are reservoirs of air, and air is the lord of strength. Whoever speaks of strength must know air—this is a universal truth. Good lungs equal good strength; weak lungs, weak strength. You must learn to breathe properly. Many years ago the boxers of the North

* The author here reveals the rigorousness of the practice in those times. Two hours of foothold practice for a beginner would be killing. Nowadays, 15 minutes would be considered more realistic. (ed.)

put breathing first as a prerequisite for gaining physical power. The achievement they made is evident today. A weak person after ten years of breathing practice can lift a load weighing 1,000 pounds! Breathing brings strength to the hands.

The boxers of the South used to practice the foothold exercise, but few of them practiced breathing. This was because the internal organs could be damaged through improper breathing. It was not until Monk Hui Meng's arrival in the South (late Ming dynasty, A.D. 1368–1644) that the boxers there learned the secrets of breathing. After his arrival they began to couple the foothold exercise with the breathing practice, thereby making their art more complete.

The breathing taught by Hui Meng had four taboos:

a. *Initially, do not overdo.* At first 49 inhalation-exhalation cycles are quite enough for an exercise period. Gradually increase the number, but on no account do over 100 cycles during a single period.

b. *Dusty or dirty premises must not be used.* It is most suitable to practice breathing in the morning in some quiet, well-ventilated place. Outdoor practice should be done in the evening.

c. *The mouth should not be used for exhalation.* To start, exhale three times through the mouth. This will rid the stomach of stale air. Thereafter, every exhalation is through the nostrils.

d. *Do not allow your thoughts to ramble during practice.* If you do, it will impede the circulation of your *ch'i* and blood. Your thought must be focused on the exercise; otherwise progress will not come.

These four taboos must be avoided. With progress your sinews will gain pliability and your entire body will become stronger. *Ch'i* and blood will flow in perfect harmony with your breathing. Then you will be able to direct your *ch'i* to any part of your body in a fraction of a second. Your will directs your *ch'i,* which is accompanied by strength. Then, just a touch on your enemy may prove fatal. *Ch'i* is truly mysterious and divine!

Another great teacher, Monk Hung Hui, has revealed that *ch'i* can be a shield for almost any part of the body. A boxer can direct his *ch'i* to his head, chest, abdomen, etc., and even a blow with an iron bar at that point will not cause pain.

As stated earlier, the art of breathing prevailed in the North in the two schools, the Hsichiang and the Honan. A basic secret of their practice stressed long exhalation and short inhalation. Essentially, it consists of, first, standing upright and exhaling the stale air three times through the mouth. Then the student bends at the waist and extends his arms directly downward. Following this, he clasps his hands and lifts them as though he were lifting a load of 1,000 pounds. During this movement he directs his *ch'i* to his navel and arms by inhaling. Then, standing upright, he shoots the left and then the right open hand forward, expelling a breath through the mouth as he does, so as to avoid any side effect.

Next he may shoot his arms upward or out to the sides, the objective always being to promote the circulation of *ch'i*. When he shoots his arms upward, he feels the *ch'i* go to the armpits and then down to the very tips of the fingers; when they go to the sides his navel is full of *ch'i*. In bringing his arms back to his sides, he closes his hands and pulls as if against a heavy load. Constancy is the key word here. Progress comes gradually with patience.

Hard and Soft

Although boxing is just a branch of the combat arts, mastery can be graded—as can Buddhist accomplishment—to three levels. The three grades for boxers are based on their ability in the hard and soft. The best boxer is neither hard nor soft but, at the same moment, both. The enemy cannot anticipate his action; his movements are beyond detection. His fingers look soft, but when they touch they feel like chisels or drills. Even when the enemy is hurt he cannot tell how and whence the attack came. In short the greatest boxer looks and acts soft, but the softness, when used, achieves results usually associated with prodigious strength or hardness. This Grade One art cannot be gained in a short period.

A Grade Two boxer is considerably inferior to a Grade One boxer. Often a student, gifted and exceptional in every way, ends at this level simply for want of a good teacher. He cannot harmonize the hard and soft. He may be taught wrongly to use drugs for his training. He may develop a part of his body which, although powerful, is disproportionate to the whole, thereby affecting overall use. His enemies may be frightened by his outwardly powerful appearance, but

when he meets a Grade One boxer his deadened muscles cannot compete with the soft maneuverings of his adversary. What then is the use of the hardened part? The Grade Two boxer lacks knowledge of the harmonious combination of soft and hard. A boxer steeped primarily in the hard takes arbitrary actions. He knows little of the foothold and less of correct breathing, the twin prerequisites of success. He cannot harmonize the substantial and the insubstantial. Since he depends solely on the strength of his arms and legs, his final accomplishment is low. Beginners should not be impressed by this level of skill.

The Grade Three boxer is even worse. His is a deplorable case. Even an excellent teacher can do little with him once his habits are fixed. This boxer is overdeveloped physically to the detriment of the coordinated action of his entire body. Whereas the Grade Two boxer fails by having too much hard and too little soft, the Grade Three boxer knows only the hard. The following four are exercises typical of this lower grade:

1. *Planting fingers in sand.* This thrusting practice is common, the aim being to make the fingers as strong as iron.

2. *Kicking a stake.* By sweeping a stake imbedded deeply

in earth, one's feet are supposed to benefit. This practice formerly was popular in Kwangtung.

3. *Plucking nails*. Using only the fingertips, the student attempts to extricate nails driven into a board. This too was popular in Kwangtung.

4. *Grinding palms*. The student is taught to rub the rims of the palms against table edges until calluses form. Then he grinds the rims on stones until they are like iron. Such a palm appears terrible to laymen but is nothing to a soft boxer.

In conclusion, the Grade One art requires harmony between the soft and hard; the Grade Two art overstresses the hard; and the Grade Three art knows only the hard.

Five Prerequisites

To harmonize the hard and soft, much depends on a correct beginning. Five rules are prescribed.

1. *Gradual Progress*. The learner must start slowly. If initial practice is conducted too vigorously the internal organs may suffer and the externals be subjected to great pain. Boxing has a bad reputation because of the number of casualties resulting from doing too much too soon. Many

resulted from exhibitionist displays of muscle. Almost all such defects can be attributed to the lack of a good teacher. As Monk Ting Hsing aptly said: "Boxing is meant to prolong life, not shorten it."

2. *Constancy the Key to Success.* Many are interested in boxing, and not a few claim some skill in the art, but only one out of a thousand really achieves success. Why is this? Simply because most boxers lack perseverance. If a person persists in daily practice he can gain some success in three years and possibly become a great boxer in 10 years. Surely it is worth the effort. For skill brings health, confidence, and happiness.

3. *Moderation a Must.* Before starting his training a man's body is insipid; afterward it becomes energized and active. Lustful desires and an affinity for alcohol destroy what has been accomplished. If one likes to indulge himself it is better that he not begin. Young people especially must pay heed to this requirement.

4. *A Peaceful Nature Should Be Cultivated.* An expert boxer is not bellicose and egotistic. He is calm and quiet, a man of leniency and patience.

5. *Customs and Regulations Must Be Observed.* Although

Ta Mo founded our boxing, others developed it and brought it to fruition. By the end of the Ming dynasty it had spread to the South. Certain customs and regulations were devised. In encountering an opponent you must go back three steps and then forward a step and a half. Then you place your right palm over your left fist. If your opponent is of the same school, a fight is thus avoided. Every Shaolin boxer observes this recognition custom.

The Ten Commandments

These regulations were established by Monk Chueh Yuan after abuses began to creep into Shaolin. They aimed to put an ethical floor under the system and to improve the discipline.

1. A student must practice without interruption.
2. Boxing must be used only for legitimate self defense.
3. Courtesy and prudence must be shown all teachers and elders.
4. A student must be forever kind, honest, and friendly to all his colleagues.
5. In traveling, a boxer should refrain from showing his

art to the common people even to the extent of refusing
challenges.

6. A boxer must never be bellicose.

7. Wine and meat must never be tasted.

8. Sexual desire cannot be permitted.

9. Boxing should not be taught rashly to non-Buddhists
lest it produce harm. It can only be transmitted to one who
is gentle and merciful.

10. A boxer must eschew aggressiveness, greed, and
boasting.

3

The Technique

IT is not difficult to learn boxing but it is extremely difficult to become expert. I have practiced for 29 years, traveled extensively, and met scores of great boxers. In Shensi, Shantung, Hopei, Shansi, Honan, and Szechwan there are many proficient boxers, especially in the Shensi-Shansi and Shansi-Shantung borderlands.

Although they teach in different ways, one can separate the art into schools of the North and of the South. Both North and South have excellent methods—neither should be depreciated. Some boxers are skilled in finger work, some in the leg art, while others devote themselves almost solely to breathing. Still others are adept at jumping. They look like a profusion of flowers in full bloom. Sometimes one is puzzled by their mysterious and incomprehensible techniques. One must have a good teacher to lead him through this plethora.

When I meet a good boxer I watch closely and find out the school to which he belongs. I conceal what I know so as to elicit greater information from him. After years of study, I must observe that most schools and techniques are based on certain common principles.

Figure 21. Circling Hand

The Foothold

The posture of the horse-riding stance was essentially the same in the North and South although different names were used. The foothold is important in that your *ch'i* is held in your lower torso. If your *ch'i* floats, your upper body will be heavier, you will pant, and your feet will be unstable.

In training for the foothold you must hold your body low and your back straight. Do not surrender to the pain, standing upright often to relieve yourself. Persist and punish yourself. Hold your head and neck straight and look straight ahead.

The Hand

Generally, finesse in the hand art stems from Warrior Yueh (Sung dynasty, A.D. 960–1280). In the North the long hand is stressed for great hand strength, and in the South they prize the short hand for protective purposes. In normal training the long hand is good for spreading the *ch'i,* but in actual combat the short hand is necessary. Thus you should harmonize the two.

1. *Circling Hand.* Both hands are used for circular interception whether frontally or laterally. Frontally, if an enemy

attacks you, retreat directly backward a step to avoid his attack and immediately step forward with your hands hitting out. Because this version resembles the attack of a monkey it is often called Monkey Hand. Laterally, your circling arms deflect his direct attack to the side. This method requires dexterity and speed. (See Figure 21.)

2. *Deflecting Hand*. One hand is used for warding off and the other for instantaneous attack (Figure 22). Two other methods of deflection are illustrated in Figures 23 and 24.

3. *Separate Short-Long Dragon Hand*. The Northern school likes this style very much. However, it must be done speedily so that once your opponent's balance is broken he not be allowed to recover and counter (Figure 25).

4. *Scissor Hand*. Use one palm downward for deflecting and the other upward to scissor the blocked fist or hand (Figure 26). As you use it, turn your body slightly sidewise and keep your chest inward so as to avoid the pressure of the attack and also give yourself space to move in countering. This method is effective in blunting the enemy's attack and in opening him up for your counter. Once I met a first rate scissors specialist in the Szechwan-Kweichow area. I saw him cross his hands once and his adversary suffered a

Figure 22. Deflecting Hand

Figure 23. Deflecting Hand: Variation

Figure 24. Deflecting Hand: Variation

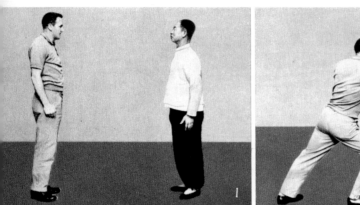

Figure 25. Separate Short-Long Dragon Hand

Figure 26. Scissor Hand

Figure 27. Cutting Hand

broken arm. The scissor hand may cross at either the elbow or the wrist of the opponent. Varieties of the technique are to use both palms downward or upward.

5. *Cutting Hand.* This is similar to the Scissor Hand, in which both palms are downward. However, the hands may be employed singly as well as together. When one hand is used it cuts at the vital points of the enemy. As in the Scissor Hand, you can mobilize greater strength if you stand laterally to your opponent. (See Figure 27.)

6. *Upholding Hand.* Upholding is done with the palm

Figure 28. Upholding Hand

flatly upward as if you were holding a plate in front while the rear hand hooks the enemy's opposite hand outward (Figure 28). If delivered smartly, it can injure the enemy while the hooking hand deflects his subsequent attack and unbalances him.

7. *Pointing Hand.* This can be done by one finger or by several used together (Figure 29). Without extensive work in cultivating *ch'i,* however, success will not come. The one-finger thrust is the most difficult one, and only a few boxers ever gained fame for it. It is the zenith of the art. Five years'

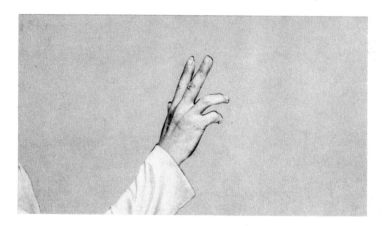

Figure 29. Pointing Hand

practice will not bring it. My teacher once told me that in the Kueichow-Yunnan area a man surnamed Hu spent 50 years perfecting this art. He was a convoy guard for some opium smugglers and thus was able to travel widely proving his art. He was over 70 when hired as a guard and was truly unbeatable. Once a score of armed hoodlums attacked him in a teahouse and Hu was able to deflect their weapons and defeat them soundly through sole use of the one finger! My teacher saw this happen and praised Hu's art as divine.

8. *Restraining Hand.* There are various ways of seizing and imprisoning the opponent's arms (Figures 30–32). These usually include or are followed by an unbalancing action and attack. Such techniques are useful for beginners, but against an experienced boxer who can paralyze with one blow they avail not. Some there are, however, who have made a great science of this. Hsiung Ch'ien-nan, a famous Hsichiang boxer, said before his death that this tactic was peerless if one knew the precise location of the fatal points on a human and knew the time when the blood passed certain junctions. For over a century this art has languished, and few if any are masters of it today.

9. *General Advice.* The eight hand methods enumerated

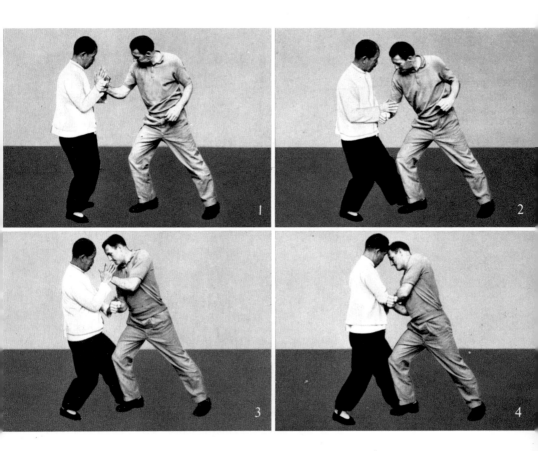

Figure 30. Restraining Hand

above are a mere introduction. Actually, a good boxer will not be deterred by some of these, notably the Cutting Hand. If two excellent boxers meet, victory will be determined by their ability to change. If equal on changes, victory will hinge on agility. If equal on agility, victory will be decided on ingenuity. If equal on ingenuity, then victory will go to the one with greater overall ability.

So you may rightly ask: is it necessary to learn the Cutting Hand? Yes, for there are times when it is useful. It is especially useful against a boxer who knows only the hard and

Figure 31.   Restraining Hand: Variation

cannot distinguish the soft. This type can be recognized because he:

a. holds his fists too high and exposes the armpit(s).

b. withdraws his arm awkwardly after an attack, thus
exposing himself to injury.

c. stands without a horse-riding posture; in this wise he
has as much stability as a tomb.

d. uses his temper and does not control his actions.

Against such a one the Cutting Hand cannot fail. But against

Figure 32. Restraining Hand: Variation

a veteran whose actions are too subtle for you to diagnose, this action will not work.

Here are some general rules for hand use.

a. Deflect and Uphold against an attack from above.

b. Use a Cutting Hand against a low attack.

c. A Restraining Hand is best used against a horizontal attack.

d. If attacked head-on fiercely, counter fiercely but laterally rather than directly forward.

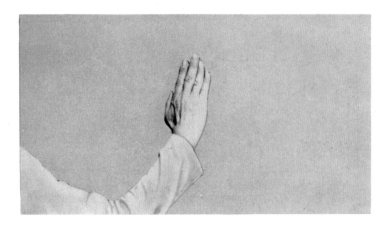

Figure 33. Willow-Leaf Palm

e. Use your enemy's strength to defeat him. Veterans say: "A strength of 1,000 pounds can be repulsed with four ounces."

f. If the enemy is strong attack laterally; if weak, strike frontally.

g. If an enemy grabs you from behind, make a horse-riding posture and bump your head against his nose. Failing this, bring a heel into his groin. Or inhale, work your arms loose, and elbow his solar plexus. But these are for children ...a veteran would never be caught in this way.

In sum, hand operation has many varieties. At first learn a little of all. Later choose one method as a specialty and devote yourself to it. Academic research is the same: you go from the general to the specific. My teacher often said: "The simpler the method, the better it is." After you specialize, spurn the other varieties. Stick to the one with constancy and perfection will come.

The Palm

The Northern school made great use of the palm. They stressed the close combination of the four fingers with the thumb curved and attached to the palm edge in the Willow

Figure 34. Tiger's Claws Palm

Leaf Palm (Figure 33). Monk Pan Hui's method was to hook the four fingers in the so-called Tiger's Claws (Figure 34). This was the style which became popular in the South. The two methods mobilize strength from the center of the palm outward.

To learn how to use the palms we must heed the advice of Yueh Wu-mu (Sung dynasty), famed for his two-hand pushing. The *ch'i* must disperse from the shoulders and be centralized in the palms. The best target is the rib cage (Figure 35), but there are many others (Figures 36 and 37).

Figure 35. Palm Attack to Rib Cage

You can use either one palm alone or both palms conjoined, but you must attack at the right time.

Monk Pan Hui learned the palm method for over 20 years. His teaching is embodied in the following verse:

Ch'i goes from the navel part,
Strength centers in the palm heart;
In the substantial your strength is found.
Exhale air while making a sound.
Upward pushing is necessary;

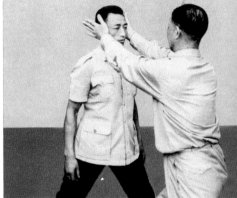

Figure 36. Palm Attack to Groin   *Figure 37.* Palm Attack to Ears

Pressing with a horse step, primary.
Remember Attacking, Pushing, and Blowing (Exhaling),
The bones near your pulses are forcefully going.

Boxer T'ieh Chai-shih once commented: "The palm operation first depends on the use of the fingers. After shooting your fingers to the enemy's throat, press the base of your palm down flat. When you feel your strength focused in the palm against his right spot, you let your palm go with full strength as you exhale with a shout. But this is a dangerous method. Only use it in an emergency."

The Wrist and Elbow

My teacher told me: "Exercise which does not involve the entire body is harmful. To overexercise one part initially can be injurious. Therefore, deal with the whole body and then specialize. Even when you accomplish the whole don't neglect it in favor of overspecialization on one part."

The practice on wrists and elbows belongs to the Scissor Hand (Figures 38 and 39). The strength from under your armpits is equally divided. Keep in mind two things:

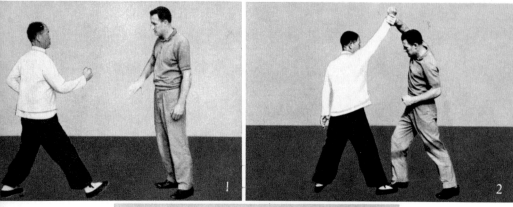

Figure 38. Elbow Attack

1. Use your elbow swiftly so as to negate your enemy's defense.

2. Don't go too high with your elbow or you will provide a vital opening.

Teacher Yueh Ch'iu-shih once said: "When you reach the stage in which every bone is divine, your blood and spirit go as freely as a dragon or a tiger. The two centers of your foot soles correspond with the centers of the palms. Exhalation and strength go together."

Figure 39. Elbow Attack: Variation

The Foot

In the use of the feet—and there are hundreds of methods —the admonitions of the earliest masters hold. The feet should be employed stealthily and speedily. Counters must be anticipated. Though low kicks are the best, occasionally a higher kick may be in order. Seldom, however, does it go as high as the head. The feet should always be used in conjunction with the hands and preferably in a countering rather than a leading role. See Figures 40–43 for examples of various foot techniques.

The Posture

The foothold and hand and palm exercises may take up 50 to 60 percent of your time initially. The correct use of the body *as a unit* is the bridge between this practice and high skill. First you learn the proper way to advance, retreat, rise, and sink. Gradually, agility comes. The various body postures are explained in such styles as the Dragon, Tiger, Leopard, Snake, and Crane, which you can master through diligent study and practice. Ideas common to both North and South are discussed briefly below.

1. *Advancing and Retreating.* To advance or retreat is a

Figure 40. Foot Attack

Figure 41. Foot Attack: Variation

Figure 42. Foot Attack:
Variation

Figure 43. Foot Attack:
Variation

matter of a second. Some advance or retreat with a step; others with a jump of 10 feet. The same applies to lateral movement. In going laterally you may step in front of or to the rear of the opposite foot. Sometimes an apparent advance is used to cover an intended withdrawal. Similarly, a seemingly unsubstantial step may turn out to be substantial.

When you fail to hit the enemy, retreat a step—this gives you an opportunity to attack again. The leading boxers in Szechwan and Kweichow taught their students the following:

> Advance with the wind's speed,
> Withdraw after the violent deed.
> Go ahead again with body sidelong,
> Don't mind a little pushing on.
> Shoot a power palm while exhaling,
> For effectiveness a shout entailing.
> Like a dragon move here and there,
> To win or lose is a moment's affair.

When your enemy attacks your chest, depress your chest inward in what is called the "swallow" action. You can then intercept and react. If his attack is short, the "swallow"

action is even more necessary. This posture is the result of long practice. The reverse posture of the "swallow" is used against palm actions. Then your strength is unleashed from under your armpits.

2. *Lateral Movements*. No matter how strong or experienced you are, lateral dodging is. of value. When you edge to the left you dodge from the right—these actions are one and the same.

> Edging and dodging need sharp eyesight;
> You must move fast to left and right;
> To dodging edging owes,
> From the unreal the real goes.
> A mountain slide you may escape
> By wedging ahead through the gape.
> Flinch not at actions furious;
> To beat the great with the small is truly curious.

Of course a firm foothold is necessary as is a perfect horse step which goes left or right easily. In sum, posture involves a correct foothold, advancing and retreating, and moving laterally with ease.

Sight and Sound

Sight is a primary requirement for a novice in boxing. If his sight is poor he is at a disadvantage. Summarized, the secret of successful boxing lies in sharp eyes, quick hands, steady courage, a firm step, and substantial strength.

Where should one look when fighting? It varied with the school. The Shansi school boxers watched the enemy's shoulder tips; the fighters of the Honan school, the enemy's chest. Generally, the Northerners watched the enemy's fingertips while the boxers in Szechwan, Kweichow, Hunan, and Hupei watched the eyes of their adversaries. One cannot disparage the one or the other. It is best to master all so that the proper one may be used at the proper time. When you watch it is with a lion's stare, with an eagle's sharpness. Your mind is freed of thoughts of life or death and the stare is all-embracing, functioning without the necessity for conscious thought.

Hearing is important in warding off a rear attack. Acute hearing is the result of long years of sedentary work. It is said of Ta Mo that after he faced the wall in meditation for nine years he could hear the conversation of the ants!

A Final Word

Shansi boxers say that correct hitting is invisible. The enemy should fall without seeing your hands. When you can do that this book will no longer have anything for you.

Index

posture, 63—66; *see also* horse-riding posture